A Bluestocking Guide
Ancient Rome

by
Jane A. Williams

based on Richard J. Maybury's book
ANCIENT ROME: HOW IT AFFECTS YOU TODAY

published by
Bluestocking Press

web site: www.BluestockingPress.com
Phone 800-959-8586

Copyright © 2004 by Jane A Williams

All rights reserved. No part of this book may be used, reproduced, or transmitted in any form or by any means, electronic or mechanical, including photocopying, recording, or by any informational storage or retrieval system, except by a reviewer who may quote brief passages in a review to be printed in a magazine or newspaper, without permission in writing from the author or publisher. Although the author and publisher have researched all sources to ensure the accuracy and completeness of the information contained in this book, we assume no responsibility for errors, inaccuracies, omissions, or any inconsistency herein. Any slights of people or organizations are unintentional.

Printed and bound in the United States of America.
Cover design by Brian C. Williams, El Dorado, CA
Edited by Kathryn Daniels

ISBN 0-942617-48-7

Published by

Bluestocking Press • Post Office Box 1014
Placerville, CA 95667-1014 • Phone: 800-959-8586
web site: www.BluestockingPress.com

Quantity Discounts Available

Books published by Bluestocking Press are available at special quantity discounts for bulk purchases to individuals, businesses, schools, libraries, and associations, to be distributed as gifts, premiums, or as fund raisers.

For terms and discount schedule contact:

Special Sales Department
Bluestocking Press
Phone: 800-959-8586
email: CustomerService@BluestockingPress.com
web site: www.BluestockingPress.com

Specify how books are to be distributed: for classrooms, or as gifts, premiums, fund raisers — or to be resold.

Contents

How to Use This Guide 4
How to Grade Assignments 6

Chapter Title	Questions	Answers

Uncle Eric's Model of How the World Works 7 30
Author's Disclosure 9 32
Thought Questions 10 32
Ancient Rome Timeline 11 33

 1. History Repeats 12 33
 2. The Roman Disease that Stalks the Markets ... 13 34
 3. The Roman Model 15 35
 4. Hitler and Mussolini 17 37
 5. The Roman Lust for Blood 18 39
 6. Logic vs. Interests 19 39
 7. Listen to the Music 20 40
 8. The Return to Feudalism 21 40
 9. Straight Lines 22 41
10. The Byzantine Empire 23 42
11. Summary 25 44

Final Exam 27 45

How to Use This Guide

Bluestocking Guides are designed to reinforce and enhance a student's understanding of the subject presented in the primer. The subject for this study guide is Ancient Rome. The primer is ANCIENT ROME: HOW IT AFFECTS YOU TODAY by Richard J. Maybury.

Given the wide range of age and ability levels of individuals who read ANCIENT ROME: HOW IT AFFECTS YOU TODAY, it is suggested that students complete the exercises in this study guide that are most age-appropriate or ability-appropriate for them.

Assignment of Exercises

While all given questions and assignments are designed to enhance the student's understanding and retention of the subject matter presented in the primer, it is by no means mandatory that each student complete every exercise in this study guide. This study guide is designed for flexibility based on a student's age, as well as a student's interest in the material presented.

It is strongly suggested that each student complete the Comprehension Exercises, but instructors can preview and then select the Application Exercises, Films to View, and Suggested Books to Read that they wish the student to complete, based on: course time available, student's interest, and/or student's age (some films/books might not be age appropriate — the student might be too young, too old, or the content too advanced for a younger student). Also, depending on the age and interest level of a student, one student might spend weeks on a research assignment, whereas another student might spend a few hours or days.

Suggested Time Frame For Study

This study guide is organized to allow the instructor flexibility in designing the ideal course of study. Therefore, there is no "right" or "wrong" time frame for covering the material; the instructor should tailor the study of the primer and study guide to the student's unique school schedule, learning style, and age. For example, younger students may only complete comprehension exercises, whereas older students may complete additional application exercises, suggested readings, and films.

An easy-to-apply rule of thumb for determining length of study is to divide the number of chapters in a primer by the number of weeks the instructor plans to study the subject/book.

Ideally, the student should read a chapter from the primer and then immediately answer the corresponding questions in the study guide. Chapter length varies, so sometimes a student may be able to read more than one chapter and complete the corresponding questions/exercises in a day. Some instructors may choose to complete the primer in a few short weeks in which case multiple chapters per day will need to be covered. Others may plan to study the primer over an entire semester, so only a few chapters per week will be assigned. The key is to move quickly enough that the student is engaged with learning and also able to absorb all concepts fully. The student's performance on end-of-chapter Questions and Assignments should be a good indication of this.

The time frame for completing application exercises (Discussion/Essay/Assignment/Research) is also subject to the instructor's discretion. Most discussions can take place immediately after reading the chapter. However, students may need a day or two to complete an essay, and some assignments will take outside research requiring additional time. It is best for the instructor to preview the application exercises (Discussion/Essay/Assignment/Research) and assign the student a "due date" based upon the student's cognitive abilities and available course schedule.

How to Use This Guide

Comprehension Exercises

Comprehension Exercises test the degree to which the student understands and retains the information presented in each chapter. In this study guide Comprehension Exercises include: 1) Define, 2) True/False, and 3) Short Answer/Fill-In. Students are encouraged to answer all exercises in complete sentences. The information needed to complete these exercises can usually be found in the given chapter of the primer. Answers will be found in the answer section of this Study Guide.

Define

The student should define the given term based on Richard Maybury's definition provided in the given chapter or glossary (*not* a standard dictionary definition). This is essential. As Richard Maybury says, "Fuzzy language causes fuzzy thinking." For any discussion or explanation to be clearly understood, one must first understand the intended definition of words as used by the author. Confusion and disagreement can occur because the student does not understand the author's intended definition of a word. To reinforce this point, have a student look up the word "law" in an unabridged Webster's dictionary. The student should find a number of definitions following the word "law." Again, unless one agrees on the definition intended for the discussion or study at hand, misunderstanding or "fuzzy thinking" can result.

True/False

For True/False exercises, if the student believes the statement is correct, the student should simply write "True" as the answer. If the student believes the statement is *not* true, the student should write "False." If the student answers the question "False," the student should be sure to state why the statement is *not* true or rewrite the false statement to make it true. In the answer section of this study guide, statements that are "False" are so noted and have been rewritten to make them true.

Short Answer/Fill In

The student should answer Short Answer/Fill In questions based upon knowledge gained from studying the given chapter. Unless the student is asked to use his/her own opinion or knowledge, the answer should be based upon Richard Maybury's statements. Generally, Short Answer/Fill In Questions are selected verbatim from the given chapter.

Application Exercises

With few exceptions, Application Exercises ask the student to apply the knowledge and ideas he/she has gained from a given chapter to "real world" situations. In many cases, these assignments are designed to help the student personalize the information just learned so that the student can better retain and apply the knowledge. In this study guide application exercises include: 1) Discussion, 2) Essay, 3) Assignment, and 4) For Further Research. In the majority of instances, answers to Application Exercises will vary based upon the student's own experiences. Application Exercises are designed to encourage informal discussions among students and instructors, and/or to stimulate students to critically evaluate the scenario. However, the instructor may ask the student to write answers (in essay format, outline, etc.) if a more formal/structure approach is desired.

For Further Reading or To View

The books and films mentioned in For Further Reading and To View are designed to expand students' understanding of concepts presented in the related chapter. No written or verbal reports on the books/movies are usually required, however, students and instructors are encouraged to discuss the ideas presented. Thus, Suggestions for Further Reading/Viewing usually have no set answers and, therefore, may not appear in the "Answer" section. (The instructor may choose to assign a book/movie report of his/her own construction if he/she desires.)

How to Grade Assignments

Define, True/False, Short Answer/Fill-In

To determine the percentage of correct answers, divide the total number of correct answers by the total number of questions. If, for example, a chapter section has two Define questions, one True/False question, and seven Short Answer/Fill-In questions, and the student has answered correctly eight of these questions, the student will have answered 80% of the questions correctly.

$$8 \div 10 = .80 \text{ (or 80\%)}$$

Number of Correct Answers ÷ Number of Total Questions = Percentage of Questions Answered Correctly

In "Grade" equivalents, percentage scores generally range as follows:

```
90 - 100%    = A
80 - 89.9%   = B
70 - 79.9%   = C
60 - 69.9%   = D
less than 60% = F
```

In general, a student earning an "A" has demonstrated excellent understanding of the subject matter; a student earning a "B" has demonstrated good understanding of the subject matter; a student earning a "C" has demonstrated sufficient understanding of the subject matter; and a student earning a "D" or "F" would benefit from reviewing the subject matter to strengthen his/her understanding of the topic at hand.

In determining whether a student has provided a "right" or "wrong" answer to a question, the instructor should compare the student's answers with the answers provided in this guide. True/False, Fill-In, and Define questions/answers are straightforward. Short Answer questions/answers are also generally straightforward; on some longer answers the student's wording may vary slightly from the answer provided in this study guide, but the student should receive full credit if the *content* of his/her answer is correct. When in doubt, it is recommended that the instructor refer back to the chapter in the primary text to reference what the author said about the issue at hand.

"Answers Will Vary"

In the answer section of this study guide you will sometimes come across an answer that reads "answers will vary" for a given question. This generally means that the student is required to answer the question using his/her own knowledge, experience, or intuition. In these instances, the instructor should refer back to the chapter in the primary text to reference what the author said about the issue at hand compared to the student's answer; a "correct" answer should be thoughtful, complete, and on-topic.

Discussion/Essay/Assignment

These assignments are provided so that students can apply the concepts they learned in the given chapter to their own experiences, current events, or historical events — to make the concepts more meaningful. In most cases, it is extremely difficult to "grade" the completed assignments as "right" or "wrong." Instead, the instructor should provide guidance for these assignments. The completeness, thoughtfulness, enthusiasm, and meaning the student brings to the assignment will serve as an indication of the student's mastery of the assignment. If the instructor then wishes to assign a grade, he/she may elect to do so. Or, these assignments may be non-graded "extra credit," serving to boost the student's overall grade for the course.

Uncle Eric's Model of How the World Works

Short Answer/Fill-in/True or False

1. What is a model as defined by Uncle Eric?

2. According to Uncle Eric, why are models important?

3. Why is it important to sort incoming data?

4. Are models rigid? Should they ever change?

5. What are the two models Uncle Eric believes are most reliable, as well as crucially important for everyone to learn? Why does he believe this?

6. _____ is the political philosophy that is no philosophy at all. It embraces the concept that those in power can do whatever appears necessary to achieve their goals.

Discussion/Essay/Assignment

7. Other than Uncle Eric's model, can you provide other examples of models?

8. What purpose does the book ANCIENT ROME: HOW IT AFFECTS YOU TODAY have relative to Uncle Eric's Model?

9. Listen to, or read, politicians' political speeches, news conferences, news releases, etc., and note if, or how often, the politicians use the phrase "we will do whatever is necessary" to execute a proposal, fix a problem, etc. Do you think it is ever okay to "do whatever is necessary" to resolve a problem? Explain your answer.

10. Look up several of the following words in a dictionary and read their definitions: fascism, liberty, economics, history, republic, and democracy. Does each word have more than one definition? Why?

11. If a word has more than one definition, why is it important that an author define his/her meaning of a word about which he/she is writing?

12. Richard Feynman, a Nobel prize winning physicist, once said it didn't matter what something was called, so long as one understood the characteristics that go into making up what that thing is. It doesn't matter if we call the bird identified as a Blue Jay, "a Blue Jay," so long as we understand that the living creature called by that name has the following characteristics: The bird's food consists primarily of nuts and small seeds as well as insects. They lay from three to six eggs that are blue, green, or yellow with spots of brown or gray. They live for about four years. Another example might be: You might have different names

during your lifetime, but you are still the same person. When you are born your parents might name you William. As a child, you might be Billy, or you might be given a nickname (i.e. Laura Ingalls Wilder from the LITTLE HOUSE™ books was called Half-pint by her Pa). As a teenager you might be Bill or Will, then, as an adult, you might use the more formal William. In all these cases, with all these names, you are still you. If you are female, you might have a maiden name and a married name. Do you agree or disagree with Richard Feynman? Does it matter what something is called, so long as one understands the characteristics of the thing? Explain and provide support for your position.

For Further Reading

13. Read ARE YOU LIBERAL? CONSERVATIVE? OR CONFUSED? by Richard J. Maybury for additional information on fascism and other political philosophies. Published by Bluestocking Press, web site: www.BluestockingPress.com; Phone: 800-959-8586.

14. Read CAPITALISM FOR KIDS by Karl Hess for additional information on different political philosophies, particularly the chapter called "Capitalism and Other Isms." Published by Bluestocking Press, web site: www.BluestockingPress.com; Phone: 800-959-8586.

Author's Disclosure

Short Answer/Fill-in/True or False

1. What is Juris Naturalism?

Discussion/Essay/Assignment

2. In the "Author's Disclosure" Richard Maybury says that few writers disclose the viewpoints or opinions they use to decide what information is important and what is not, or what data will be presented and what data omitted. Collect several history books from your home library, school library, or public library. Do the authors of the books you collected disclose their viewpoints or opinions to the reader? Do the authors disclose what criteria they used to determine what information or data to include in the book and what to omit? Explain why it is, or is not, important to have biases disclosed. What benefit, if any, does a reader or viewer have (in the case of movies, televised news, or documentaries) if he/she is able to determine the viewpoint of a writer?

3. Uncle Eric says all history is slanted based on the facts historians choose to report. Can you provide examples of material you have read or to which you have listened where facts have been reported but perhaps not all the facts? If no books come to mind, have you had arguments or disagreements between siblings or friends in which, when asked, each person presented his/her side of the argument—presenting only those facts that best favored his/her side of the story? How can you learn to identify the slants of writers, news commentators, friends, etc.?

4. Read the quotes in the "Author's Disclosure" section of this book that help to describe the Juris Naturalist viewpoint. Look up the definition of "unalienable" in a current dictionary. Compare a current dictionary's definition with the definition from NOAH WEBSTER'S 1828 DICTIONARY: "Unalienable; that cannot be legally or justly alienated or transferred to another ... All men have certain natural rights which are "inalienable".

5. Samuel Adams defined the natural rights of the colonists as the right to life, liberty, and property. Why do you think "property" was changed to "happiness" in the Declaration of Independence? *(Optional exercise: You can turn this into a research exercise by researching primary source documents of America's Founders to see if you can find the answer for the change from "property" to "happiness." Provide support for your position.)*

6. Select one of the quotes from the "Author's Disclosure" section of this book and write a short essay about what the quote means to you.

For Further Reading

7. Read HOW TO LIE WITH STATISTICS by Darrell Huff, published by W.W. Norton, and distributed by Bluestocking Press, web site: www.BluestockingPress.com; Phone: 800-959-8586. Excellent book. A modern classic. Shows how statistics can distort truth. For ages 14 and up.

8. Read EVALUATING BOOKS: WHAT WOULD THOMAS JEFFERSON THINK ABOUT THIS? an "Uncle Eric" book by Richard J. Maybury. This book provides key indicators and terms to help the reader learn how to identify the slants of authors, media commentators, and others. Published by Bluestocking Press, web site: www.BluestockingPress.com; Phone: 800-959-8586. For ages 12 and up.

9. Secure a copy of WORLD PRESS REVIEW (customer service: PO Box 228, Shrub Oak, New York, 10588, Ph: 914-962-6292). As of this writing, the web site offers a free trial issue for students and educators. The web site is www.worldpressreview.org or email is letters@worldpress.org. Each printed article lists the author and his/her philosophical viewpoint, i.e., Centrist, Libertarian, Liberal, Conservative. Have someone cover up the name and philosophical identity of each author and then read the articles. Can you identify each author's philosophical viewpoint? For help with this exercise, if a student has limited knowledge of political and economic biases, the student should first read Richard J. Maybury's book ARE YOU LIBERAL? CONSERVATIVE? OR CONFUSED? published by Bluestocking Press, or wait to do this exercise until that book is read. This exercise is repeated in the study guide for that book.

Thought Questions

Before you begin to read ANCIENT ROME: HOW IT AFFECTS YOU TODAY, answer the following questions. Your answers should be based on your current knowledge and/or opinions. (If you have no knowledge of the issue/topic, say so.) Save your responses. You will revisit these questions at a later time. After you have answered the questions, you may begin to read ANCIENT ROME: HOW IT AFFECTS YOU TODAY.

1. What do you know about Ancient Rome?

2. How does the current U.S. Government compare to the U.S. Government at the time the Constitution was signed?

3. What do you know about fascism?

Ancient Rome Timeline

Short Answer/Fill-in/True or False

1. Look at the timeline that appears before Chapter One. In what year was Rome founded?

2. Name the four distinct periods that make up the rise and fall of Ancient Rome's power.

3. Roman power was at its peak during which of the four periods that make up the rise and fall of Ancient Rome's power?

Discussion/Essay/Assignment

4. Select some books on Ancient Rome from your home, school, or public library. Make a list of which books make a distinction of the four periods that make up the rise and fall of Ancient Rome's power. Make a list of those that do not. What happens to the reader's perception about Ancient Rome and its glory or fury if the author fails to draw clear distinctions about the time periods he/she is discussing?

5. Do you think the United States has the same government, economy, and legal system today that it started with in 1786? If not, when did the changes take place? Draw a timeline for the United States from its beginning in 1776 until the present. Note any distinctions on this timeline based on any changes that have taken place in its government, economics, or legal practices from 1776 to the present. Provide a name for any time period/s you choose to identify. Why did you select the divisions that you did? Or, why did you select no divisions? Why did you select the names/titles for any time periods that you identified?

Chapter 1: History Repeats

Define

1. Roman Empire:
2. Roman disease:

Short Answer/Fill-in/True or False

3. Why does Uncle Eric think so many individuals forget the history they've learned?

Discussion/Essay/Assignment

4. Can you think of an example from your own life that was a mistake the first time it happened to you, but having learned from that mistake, has helped you to avoid further mistakes? For example, perhaps when you were very young you touched a hot object (i.e., stove, iron) and learned very quickly not to repeat the action.

5. Did your parents ever give you advice based on their own experiences to help you avoid making some of the same mistakes they, or perhaps a friend of theirs, made? Give examples. Did you listen to their advice or choose not to listen? What was the result of the choice you made? Why did you fail to heed their advice? Why did you find it necessary to live the experience yourself, rather than learn from someone else's mistake?

6. The history you study in textbooks is much the same as personal history, but on a grander scale, over a greater period of time, and with more people involved. One reason to study past events is to learn from the past in an effort to improve the present and the future. Have you ever attempted to offer guidance to someone based on your own experiences? Did the person follow your advice? Do you know why, or why not? How important is it for the advice seeker to have a trust in the reliability/credibility of the advisor?

7. Do you agree or disagree with the statement by Uncle Eric that "our present is the result of the past, and our future will be the result of the present?" Explain your answer.

8. Write your own personal history from your earliest memories to the present. Focus on those experiences from your past that have influenced current choices or future plans.

For Further Reading

9. For examples of how past actions affect current events, read Richard Maybury's World War series ("Uncle Eric" books): THE THOUSAND YEAR WAR IN THE MIDEAST AND HOW IT AFFECTS YOU TODAY; WORLD WAR I: THE REST OF THE STORY AND HOW IT AFFECTS YOU TODAY; and WORLD WAR II: THE REST OF THE STORY AND HOW IT AFFECTS YOU TODAY, published by Bluestocking Press, web site: www.BluestockingPress.com, phone: 800-959-8586. These books show how events thousands of years ago can sometimes affect us more than events in our own hometowns today. It is suggested you read these books after finishing this book.

Chapter 2: The Roman Disease That Stalks the Markets

Define

1. Fascism:
2. Roman law:
3. Statism:
4. Pax Romana:
5. Political unity:

Short Answer/Fill-in/True or False

6. According to Uncle Eric, how are investment values determined? (Circle the letter of the correct answer.)

    a. Investment values determine economic trends, which determine politics.

    b. Investment values are mostly determined by trends in the economy, and trends in the economy are determined mostly by politics.

    c. Economic trends determine politics, which determine investment values.

7. The _____ is the term coined by Uncle Eric for the political trend that has dominated the world for 2,000 years.

8. Explain/define the political trend that has dominated the world for 2,000 years. What is its basic premise?

9. What does *E Pluribus Unum* mean? On what coins is this found and why is it significant?

10. What is a fasces and on what U.S. coin is it found? What is its significance?

11. What is significant about the architecture of the Lincoln Memorial relative to Ancient Rome? (The Lincoln Memorial can be seen on the back of a penny.)

12. Define Roman Law during the Roman Empire and compare the intent of Roman Law to the intent found in the following two quotes:

    "... all men are created equal ... they are endowed by their Creator with certain unalienable rights." —Declaration of Independence, 1776

    "The natural rights of the colonists are these: first, a right to life; second to liberty; third to property; together with the right to support and defend them in the best manner they can." —Samuel Adams, 1771

13. What is the basic premise of statism?

14. What is the Pax Romana?

Discussion/Essay/Assignment

15. Watch for the fasces in architecture, art, currency, etc. Keep a list of where you see the fasces and the year it was originally used in the items.

16. Read a biography or biographical account of: 1) Russia's Peter the Great, or 2) Alexander of Macedonia and Greece. Does the author of the biography present these individuals in a positive or negative light? How can you determine an author's philosophical slant? (A good resource tool for this is Richard Maybury's EVALUATING BOOKS: WHAT WOULD THOMAS JEFFERSON THINK ABOUT THIS? published by Bluestocking Press, phone: 800-959-8586, web site: www.BluestockingPress.com

To View

17. FALL OF THE ROMAN EMPIRE, directed by Anthony Mann, starring Alec Guinness, James Mason, Christopher Plummer, and more. 1964.

Chapter 3: The Roman Model

Define

1. Kaiser:
2. Czar:
3. Caesar:
4. Roman model:
5. Common law:
6. Augur:
7. Inauguration:

Short Answer/Fill-in/True or False

8. Why can't business people plan ahead under the Roman model?

9. In the United States, what is the significance of Common law?

10. _____ hates political power and tries to neutralize it.
    _____ embraces political power and seeks to expand it.

11. What was the last great common law event in the 20th century? Why was this significant?

12. Explain the origin of the term "inaugurated."

13. In what year was the fasces removed from the dime? Why?

14. Roman Law is the basis of fascism. Roman Law allows a government to make up whatever laws it chooses. What restraints on government power does Roman Law permit?

Discussion/Essay/Assignment

15. Give an example of Roman Law in the United States.

16. Uncle Eric says that most politicians today make decisions on the basis of the Roman model. Do you think today's politicians want a strong central government that can tax and control almost everything and fight wars anywhere on earth? How many politicians can you identify/name that are not trying to legislate some aspect of your life, your money, your property, your freedom? Do not rely on what is said during a speech, a debate, or a campaign pledge or promise; rather, go to the voting records and see how your politician of choice has actually voted. Can you identify a politician who is trying to pass legislation that will take control from government and return it to the individual? A good place to begin your research is by visiting these web sites:
    http://4government.4anything.com/
    http://www.archives.gov/index.html

17. Pretend the following situation has occurred in your household: Your parents provide you an allowance of $5.00 per week. To receive that allowance you must do certain chores—take out the garbage, do the dishes, wash the car. You are a very busy person and you allocate a total of 7 hours per week, one hour per day, to complete these chores. You also decide you want to save your allowance to attend a concert which will cost you $45.00 for the ticket, which is a group rate because you and your friends have committed to go together so you can obtain the less expensive group rate ticket. You figure you can save the $45.00 in 9 weeks. However, your parents begin to reevaluate and decide you are getting too old for an allowance and decide to discontinue your allowance. They say you are old enough to find a job outside the home. You explain to your parents that you and they had an understanding: you will do designated chores in exchange for an allowance. Besides, you've made plans that involve other people based on the projected allowance you are planning to receive. What might be the outcome for you if Roman Law governed your household versus a household subject to common law?

18. Refer to an encyclopedia or the Internet and read about the United Nations. Does the description sound similar to a united government? If so, explain the similarities. If not, what are the differences between the United Nations and Ancient Rome during the Pax Romana?

19. Refer to an encyclopedia and read about the Divine Right of Kings. Ancient Rome asserted that their emperor was divine. If the emperor was granted law-making power by the Creator, then one had to assume the law was good. Is the premise correct? Does this argument have any faults?

20. Over a two-month period keep track of the number of times a government official, or anyone else, refuses to take responsibility for his/her actions because he was just following orders. How often do you hear "I was just doing my job" or "I was just following orders" given to excuse a person's actions or to pass along responsibility? Listen to the news, read the papers, look at court decisions.

21. Keeping in mind that definition of fascism is "doing whatever appears necessary," keep a record of how often you read or hear this phrase in relation to political figures, past or present. Name someone who used this term and the circumstances in which the term was used.

To View

22. Watch the movie JUDGMENT AT NUREMBURG starring Spencer Tracy for a dramatization of the last great common law event of the 20th century.

Chapter 4: Hitler and Mussolini

Define

1. Dark Ages:

2. Socialism:

Short Answer/Fill-in/True or False

3. Name the three stages of Roman civilization and give each of their dates.

4. What are the distinguishing characteristics of each of the three stages of Roman civilization?

5. Where does the Pax Romana fit within the three stages (date/circa)?

6. What is significant about the Pax Romana?

7. When did the Dark Ages begin? What was its significance?

8. Mussolini formed his fascist organization, the Fascisti, in 1919. How long did it take Mussolini to take over Italy?

9. What promise did both Mussolini and Hitler each make that helped them rise to power?

10. What is the difference in philosophy between fascism and common law?

11. America was founded on the principles of common law. What are the two laws that are taught by all major religions of the world that are the basic principles of common law?

12. Uncle Eric talks about thirteen of the most important words you will ever read. What are these words?

Discussion/Essay/Assignment

13. Listen to people, watch news, read newspapers, watch talk shows or listen to talk radio. Note how often people look to government to solve their problems. Compare this to the number of times that people look to themselves or the private sector, not government, to solve their problems.

Chapter 5: The Roman Lust for Blood

Short Answer/Fill-in/True or False

1. Why does Uncle Eric fear the former USSR will go the way of Rome and decline into a fascist system?

2. Is there a danger in believing the statement "My country right or wrong?" Explain your answer.

For Further Reading

3. Fascism assumes there is no law higher than the government's law, so fascism requires total obedience to the state. For more about Higher Law and America's common law heritage, read the "Uncle Eric" book WHATEVER HAPPENED TO JUSTICE? by Richard J. Maybury, published by Bluestocking Press, web site: www.BluestockingPress.com, phone: 800-959-8586. In this book, Maybury explains that in America Higher Law has been replaced by political law.

4. Read a biographical account of Peter the Great. In your opinion, is he a good symbol for Russia's leading "reform" party? Explain your answer.

Chapter 6: Logic vs. Interests

Short Answer/Fill-in/True or False

1. Why might governments dislike the idea of Higher Law?

2. What are vital interests, strategic interests, national interests, and general interests? What is significant about "interests"?

3. Who is Gratian and why is he important?

4. Why are the 1930s and the Great Depression significant to the history of common law?

Discussion/Essay/Assignment

5. Write an essay and provide examples to support or refute this statement: "Without a moral compass, the law becomes a destroyer."

6. Write two fictionalized accounts of two different families. Use concrete examples and applications in your story to describe life in each of the two households. The first household is governed by Roman Law, which is administered by the parents. The second household is governed by common law and all members of the household must equally abide by the Two Laws: 1) do all you have agreed to do, and 2) do not encroach on other persons or their property.

7. Listen to politicians and government officials and note if they use the term "interests" as a reason to justify action on their part.

For Further Reading

8. Read stories about the Holocaust, including the book THE OTHER VICTIMS, published by Houghton Mifflin Company, New York. Learn what groups, besides the Jewish people, were targeted by Hitler and Stalin as undesirables. For ages 12 and up.

9. Read FRIEDRICH by Hans Peter Richter, published by Puffin Penguin Books, New York. Learn how Hitler legally changed the laws in Germany in order to legally execute his ethnic cleansing program. For ages 12 and up.

Chapter 7: Listen to the Music

Short Answer/Fill-in/True or False

1. What does Chaostan mean?

2. What percentage of the earth's land does Chaostan include?

3. What is significant about the population of Chaostan?

4. What country in Europe is named after Rome?

5. What is the alternative for a civilization with no common law?

Discussion/Essay/Assignment

6. On a current European map or world globe identify the geographical area that comprises Chaostan. Remember that Chaostan is roughly the area from the Arctic Ocean to the Indian Ocean, and Poland to the Pacific, plus North Africa.

7. Uncle Eric says that the U.S. Bill of Rights stops at U.S. borders. Inside the U.S., the Bill of Rights protects individuals against the government's arbitrary use of power. Outside the U.S., the U.S. Government is not subject to the constraints of the Bill of Rights. What significance does this have for U.S. citizens that study, travel, or work abroad?

To View

8. Watch the 1964 film THE FALL OF THE ROMAN EMPIRE directed by Anthony Mann, starring Alec Guinness. The first hour reveals much about the thinking that is now popular in the former USSR, as well as NATO, the United Nations, and Washington. Per Uncle Eric's suggestion, note the emotions stirred by the film's martial music.

Chapter 8: The Return of Feudalism

Define

1. Serfdom:

Short Answer/Fill-in/True or False

2. Uncle Eric compares the fall of the Roman Empire and the dissolution of the former Soviet Empire. What conclusions does he make?

3. What is the significance of Caerphilly Castle in Wales?

Discussion/Essay/Assignment

4. After the fall of Saddam Hussein in 2003, Iraq was faced with the task of forming a new government. As I write this today, the effort in Iraq is to rebuild the government of Iraq into a democratic government. As you read this question today, what, if any, type of formal government does Iraq now have? What type of legal system, if any, did Iraq adopt (i.e., common law or political law)? What type of future might the Iraqi people have under Iraq's current political and legal system?

5. Uncle Eric says that most school textbooks teach that the Roman Empire fell because it had become militarily weak and was overrun by tribes of barbarians. He says this is a half-truth. Roman civilization had already been destroyed by socialism; the people were nearly barbarians themselves long before the arrival of foreign tribes. Try to locate some history books and see what they say caused the fall of Ancient Rome.

Chapter 9: Straight Lines

Short Answer/Fill-in/True or False

1. What is the significance of straight lines in creating borders of newly conquered lands and peoples?

2. The former Soviet Empire has different ethnic groups whose borders were changed when they were conquered. What has happened as a result of the dissolution of the former Soviet Empire?

Discussion/Essay/Assignment

3. Look at a map that shows the borders of Native American nations at the time of European impact. Do the borders of Native American nations generally fall along natural borders: rivers, lakes, and mountains? What happened when U.S. state boundaries were formed?

Chapter 10: The Byzantine Empire

Short Answer/Fill-in/True or False

1. What is the Byzantine Empire and when did it begin?

2. Who is Emperor Justinian and what is his significance?

3. What countries were the principle exceptions to Byzantine governmental rule and why?

4. Roman law, which says there is no law higher than government's law, led to the rise of fascism and WW II. It is again sparking the wars that are spreading across Chaostan. Why is everyone in Chaostan fighting for control of the government?

5. Locate Istanbul (which was Constantinople) on a map. Why did the Byzantine Empire survive when the rest of the Roman Empire couldn't?

6. What was the official religion of the Byzantine Empire prior to 1054 A.D.?

7. How did the official religion change in 1054 A.D.?

8. In 1453 the Byzantine government was so large that its large taxes, regulations, and bureaucracy brought it the same fate as the Roman Empire. Who conquered the Byzantine government and what was the religion of the conquerors?

9. Why did many cities welcome Muslims as saviors?

10. Turkey converted to Islam. Russians and Serbs were on the front lines of the Christian world against the Islamic world. Russians and Serbs became allies and fought a series of wars against the Turks. Where were the most disputed territories and why?

11. Who were the lead troops of the Russians and what was their religion?

12. Who have been the mortal enemy of the Cossacks?

13. At the beginning of the 21st century who were enemies in Bosnia, Tajikistan, the Caucasus Mountains, and Georgia?

14. What is the consistent and significant pattern among all the groups identified in the preceding question?

15. At the beginning of the 21st century what were the territories that comprised the Balkans? As you read this today, have there been any changes in these territories?

16. What is the significance of the two-headed eagle?

Discussion/Essay/Assignment

17. Two of the groups converted by the Byzantines to the Eastern Orthodox faith were the Russians and Serbs. Do you think this event more than 1,000 years ago has any impact on the fighting by the Serbs at the end of the 20th and beginning of the 21st centuries? Provide support for your position.

18. At the time of the USSR's breakup, 25 million Russians lived outside Russia in homelands of people who were once conquered by the Russians. For example, Russians were:

    23% of the population of Muslim Chechen-Ingustia
    30% of Muslim North Ossetia
    43% of Muslim Tatarstan

    These Russians were hated and persecuted. At the time you read this question, if this has been resolved, how was this accomplished? If this has not been resolved, if you were the government official in charge of resolving these conflicts, what would you do to try to achieve peace? Why do you think your plan will succeed? Provide support for your position.

For Further Reading

19. Read the section of GEORGE WASHINGTON'S FAREWELL ADDRESS in which he addresses foreign affairs. What was Washington's advice regarding America's involvement in foreign wars and foreign politics? Has America heeded his warning? Explain, and provide support for your position. Published by Applewood Books, Massachusettes. For ages 14 and up.

To View

20. Watch PBS's film ROMAN CITY. It will help you understand the Roman psychology that is behind the new wars today. Available from: web site: www.shopPBS.org or phone: 800-328-7271.

Chapter 11: Summary

Short Answer/Fill-in/True or False

1. True or False: History can seem like a meaningless collection of facts if you do not have a model of how the world works to help you understand history and learns its lessons.

2. True or False: Many people mistakenly believe the Pax Romana was the good old days and try to recreate it.

3. True or False. The Roman model is based on free markets and Higher Law principles.

4. Ancient Rome's civilization lasted about 1,250 years and was divided into three parts: Roman Republic, Roman Empire, and Roman Monarchy. What part flourished under an early form of common law?

5. _____ law was the root cause of the fall of Ancient Rome and the subsequent Dark Ages.

6. Give an example of the influence of Roman ideas and/or symbols in our civilization today.

7. _____ has been the source of history's worst wars.

8. The Roman model is also called the Roman _____ because _____.

9. True or False: The Roman model assumes political power is a bad thing.

10. What does Uncle Eric believe is fundamental to another Golden Age?

For Further Reading

11. The following list of books contain political and economic history from a perspective that is consistent with the original American philosophy that embraced free markets, Higher Law principles, and international neutrality. Those that are asterisked are "Uncle Eric" books written by Richard J. Maybury. Most are published or distributed by Bluestocking Press, web site: www.BluestockingPress.com, phone: 800-959-8586. To gain a strong foundation in America's original American philosophy, a suggested goal would be to read all these suggested books by the time you graduate high school.

*WHATEVER HAPPENED TO PENNY CANDY? by Richard J. Maybury
*WHATEVER HAPPENED TO JUSTICE? by Richard J. Maybury
*ARE YOU LIBERAL? CONSERVATIVE? OR CONFUSED? by Richard J. Maybury
*EVALUATING BOOKS: WHAT WOULD THOMAS JEFFERSON THINK ABOUT THIS? by Richard J. Maybury
*THE THOUSAND YEAR WAR IN THE MIDEAST by Richard J. Maybury
*WORLD WAR I: THE REST OF THE STORY by Richard J. Maybury
*WORLD WAR II: THE REST OF THE STORY by Richard J. Maybury
*CAPITALISM FOR KIDS by Karl Hess
THE LAW by Frederic Bastiat
THE MAINSPRING OF HUMAN PROGRESS by Henry Grady Weaver
GIVE ME LIBERTY by Rose Wilder Lane (as I write this, this book is out of print)
DISCOVERY OF FREEDOM by Rose Wilder Lane
ECONOMICS IN ONE LESSON by Henry Hazlitt

Final Exam

1. What are the two models Richard Maybury (Uncle Eric) believes are most reliable and also crucially important for everyone to learn?

2. _____ is the political philosophy that is no philosophy at all. It embraces the concept that those in power can do whatever appears necessary to achieve their goals.

3. What is Juris Naturalism?

4. In what year was Ancient Rome founded?

5. Name the four distinct periods that make up the rise and fall of Ancient Rome's power.

6. Roman power was at its peak during which of the four periods that make up the rise and fall of Ancient Rome's power?

7. What is the Roman Disease?

8. How are fasces relative to Ancient Rome?

9. What is statism?

10. How are investment values determined?

11. What is common law?

12. What restraints on government power does Roman Law permit?

13. Name the three stages of Roman civilization. What are the distinguishing characteristics of each of the three stages of Roman civilization?

14. When did the Dark Ages begin? What was its significance?

15. What are vital interests, strategic interests, national interests, and general interests? What is significant about "interests"?

16. Why are the 1930s and the Great Depression significant to the history of common law?

17. What does Chaostan mean?

18. What is significant about the population of Chaostan?

19. What are the alternatives for a civilization with no common law?

20. Define: serfdom.

21. What is the significance of straight lines in creating borders of newly conquered lands and peoples?

22. What is the Byzantine Empire and when did it begin?

23. What countries were the principle exceptions to Byzantine governmental rule and why?

24. What was the official religion of the Byzantine Empire prior to 1054 A.D.?

25. In 1453, the Byzantine government was so large that its large taxes, regulations, and bureaucracy brought it the same fate as the Roman Empire. Who conquered the Byzantine government and what was the religion of the conquerors?

26. At the beginning of the 21st century who were enemies in Bosnia, Tajikistan, the Caucasus Mountains, and Georgia?

27. True or False. The Roman model is based on free markets and Higher Law principles.

28. What does Uncle Eric believe is fundamental to another Golden Age?

29. True or False: Political law is based on fact, logic, and the two fundamental laws: 1) do all you have agreed to do, and 2) do not encroach on other persons or their property.

30. True or False: Political law is cautious and hesitant in the use of force.

31. True or False: Scientific law is predictable and knowable.

32. True or False: Political law is made up by politicians.

33. _____ law tends to neutralize political power; _____ law gives powerseekers more power.

34. _____ law uses force to redistribute wealth and destroys incentive to produce wealth.

35. True or False: Scientific law makes poor economic calculations.

36. Short Answer Essay: What are the most important points you've learned as a result of reading Ancient Rome?

Answers

Uncle Eric's Model of How the World Works

Short Answer/Fill-in/True or False

1. Uncle Eric says that models are how we think. They are how we understand how the world works.

2. According to Uncle Eric, models are important because we constantly refer to our models to help us determine what incoming data is important and what data is not.

3. It is important to sort incoming data because we need to decide what incoming data we need to remember or file for future reference, and what data we can discard, based on its importance to us, or its usefulness. We need a tool for making this determination. That tool is also called our "model."

4. This answer requires the student to draw his/her own conclusion based on the information provided in the explanation of "Uncle Eric's Model of How the World Works." Possible answer: We should always be willing to test our models against incoming data, and if our models don't stand up to the incoming data, then it becomes necessary to question and perhaps rethink our model, as well as question the reliability of the incoming data.

5. Free market economics and Higher Law are the two models Uncle Eric thinks are most reliable, as well as crucially important for everyone to learn. Free market economics and Higher Law are important models because they show how human civilization works, especially the world of money.

6. **Fascism** is the political philosophy that is no philosophy at all. It embraces the concept that those in power can do whatever appears necessary to achieve their goals.

Discussion/Essay/Assignment

7. Examples of models will vary and might include scientific models, religious models, economic models, political models, etc.

8. The book ANCIENT ROME shows what happens when a society ignores the model of free markets and Higher Law principles and embraces fascism.

9. Answers will vary.

10. Look at the front matter of your dictionary. There should be an explanation of the "Order of Definitions." For example, the order of definitions can be historical order: the earliest meaning is placed first and later meanings are arranged by semantic development.

11. The reader must understand what the author means by the words the author uses so the reader can understand the progression of the author's ideas that build on the definition of the terms used. This does not require that a reader agree with the author's definition of a word, only that the reader understand what the author means when the author uses the word. Then the reader is in a better position to critically examine the author's ideas based on a common understanding of the author's meaning.

12. Answers will vary, but might include some of the following explanations: Definitions provide clear understanding and communication between the parties involved. For example, suppose you eat a piece of fruit. This fruit happens to be a banana. Someone comes along who has never before seen or tasted a banana. With the banana in your presence, you can each begin to discuss its merits, and you will each know exactly what you're talking about. As in the Richard Feynman example, you are understanding the characteristics of the banana that go into making up what that "thing" is. To be able to give the "thing" a name, banana, that both parties can use in future communication will help promote speedier and clearer communication. This is the purpose of always making sure that you understand the definition of a term used in a discussion (whether in conversation or in books). You don't have to agree with the person's definition, but if you understand what the person means by it, you can have a clearer and more meaningful discussion instead of getting bogged down in misunderstandings regarding fuzzy language.

Author's Disclosure

Short Answer/Fill-in/True or False

1. Juris Naturalism is the belief in a Natural Law that is higher than any government's law.

Discussion/Essay/Assignment

2. Answers will vary, but students should note that the bias or philosophical slant of an author, news commentator, or reporter can influence the selection of facts included in a book or report, thereby slanting the history, or other subject areas.

3. Answers will vary.
4. Answers will vary.
5. Answers will vary.
6. Answers will vary.

Thought Questions

The student was asked to answer the following three questions before beginning to read ANCIENT ROME: HOW IT AFFECTS YOU TODAY and review these answers upon completing the book.

1. What do you know about Ancient Rome?

2. How does the current U.S. Government compare to the U.S. Government at the time the Constitution was signed?

3. What do you know about fascism?

Compare the answers before and after having read the book. Where do the responses differ and why?

Ancient Rome Timeline

Short Answer/Fill-in/True or False

1. Ancient Rome was founded circa 750 B.C.

2. The four distinct periods that make up the rise and fall of Ancient Rome's power are: Roman Monarchy, Roman Republic, Pax Romana, and the Roman Empire.

3. Roman power was at its peak during the Pax Romana.

Discussion/Essay/Assignment

4. If authors do not clearly identify the Roman time period to which they are referring, the reader is unable to determine the positives and negatives relative to Ancient Roman government, law, and economics based on the particular time period under discussion. In fact, the reader does not even know that distinctive time periods existed.

5. Answers will vary.

Chapter 1: History Repeats

Define

1. Roman Empire: The period from roughly 0 to 500 AD in Europe when statism was dominant. It was an era of rampant lawmaking, welfare statism, crushing taxes, runaway inflation, and war.

2. Roman disease: Statism. The assumption that laws can be made up by human lawmakers.

Short Answer/Fill-in/True or False

3. Uncle Eric believes most people today forget the history they've learned because they lack the tools to understand history. Without a model of economics and law people have no tools to make sense of whatever history they study and are unable to apply the lessons of history to their daily lives.

Discussion/Essay/Assignment

4-8. Answers will vary.

Chapter 2: The Roman Disease That Stalks the Markets

Define

1. Fascism: The political philosophy that is no philosophy at all, do whatever appears necessary.

2. Roman law: The legal system during the Roman Empire. It assumes the individual's rights are granted by the state (by government) and laws can be made up by lawmakers. The state is supreme, and rights are granted or erased whenever lawmakers decide.

3. Statism: The opposite of the original American philosophy. Assumes political power is a good thing and everyone should have some. Government is our friend, our protector, the solution to our problems. Force is the tool for enforcement. There is no law higher than the government's law.

4. Pax Romana: The period from 31 BC lasting about 200 years in which Rome dominated most of Europe, the Mideast, and North Africa. During the Roman Republic, the Roman common law had created great wealth so that during the period of the Pax Romana the Roman government could collect enormous taxes to finance its army, forts, and roads to conquer the whole Mediterranean world.

5. Political unity: A large, powerful government that all are forced to obey.

Short Answer/Fill-in/True or False

6. According to Uncle Eric, investment values are mostly determined by trends in the economy, and trends in the economy are determined mostly by politics.

7. The **Roman disease** is the term coined by Uncle Eric for the political trend that has dominated the world for 2,000 years.

8. The Roman disease is the assumption, like statism, that the state (government) is supreme, the individual's rights are granted by the state, and that laws can be "made up" by human lawmakers. Its basic premise is that no law is higher than the government's law.

9. E Pluribus Unum is Latin for "out of many, one." It is found on the back of these United States coins: penny, nickel, dime, quarter, and half dollar. This motto applauds political unity.

10. A fasces is found on the back of a Roosevelt dime. It is a bundle of wooden rods bound together by red-colored bands. In Ancient Rome the fasces was fixed to a wooden pole with an ax at the top or side. It symbolized the unification of the people under a single government. The ax suggested what would happen to anyone who didn't obey the government. The Roman fasces is the origin of the word fascism.

11. The style of the architecture is Greco-Roman, meaning a combination of Greek and Roman.

12. Roman Law during the Roman Empire assumes the individual's rights are granted by the state (by government) and laws can be made up by lawmakers. Under Roman Law rights are granted or erased whenever lawmakers decide. This philosophy is sometimes called statism. The quotes by Samuel Adams and from the Declaration of Independence state that individuals are endowed by their Creator with certain unalienable (natural) rights (to life, liberty, property/pursuit of happiness).

13. The basic premise of statism is that no law is higher than government's law.

14. The Pax Romana is the period in which Ancient Rome dominated the Mediterranean world. This is the time when the known world was unified, symbolized by the fasces.

Discussion/Essay/Assignment

15. Answers will vary.
16. Answers will vary.

Chapter 3: The Roman Model

Define

1. Kaiser: Means Caesar. An emperor of the German Empire.

2. Czar: Means Caesar. An emperor of the Russian Empire.

3. Caesar: An emperor of the Roman Empire.

4. Roman model: The legal system that replaced the Roman common law. Implies a large central government that all are forced to obey, that can tax and control everything, watchdog everyone's business, and fight wars anywhere on earth. Laws change continually, are arbitrary, and are not based on Higher Law principles. Statism. The opposite of common law and Natural Law.

5. Common law: The system for discovering and applying the Natural Laws that determine the results of human behavior. The system for discovering and applying the Natural Laws that govern the human ecology. The body of definitions and precedents growing from the two fundamental laws that make civilization possible: 1) do all you have agreed to do, and 2) do not encroach on other persons or their property.

6. Augur: Around 600 B.C. in Rome, a soothsayer.

7. Inauguration: To bestow with magical powers. The ceremony in which a government official is put in office either to make up laws or to enforce these laws. Dates back to about 600 B.C. Rome.

Short Answer/Fill-in/True or False

8. Business people can't plan ahead under the Roman model because the laws change continuously. The ground rules and flows of money channeled by these rules are forever changing. Legal instability brings economic instability.

9. Common law assumes there is a Higher Law than any government's law. Common law enables civilization to advance. America was founded on the common law model. Over the years it has been gradually replaced by Roman law—the supremacy of the state. Justice is whatever lawmakers say it is.

10. **Common law** hates political power and tries to neutralize it. **Roman law** embraces political power and seeks to expand it.

11. The last great common law event in the 20th century was the Nuremburg trials, 1945. The trials were significant because the Nazi defendants pled not guilty because they were just following orders of their government. The judges found them guilty, explaining there is a "higher duty" than anything our governments can impose on us.

12. Around 600 B.C. Rome, kings were chosen by a group of soothsayers called augers. The augers would "talk to the gods" and get their advice about who to make king. The king was given magical powers—inaugurated.

13. The fasces was removed from the dime in 1946. Hitler and Mussolini gave fascism a bad name.

14. There are no restraints on a government that practices Roman Law. If government can make up law, it can pass whatever laws it wants to justify whatever actions it wants to take.

Discussion/Essay/Assignment

15. An example of Roman Law in the United States was the internment of the Japanese during World War II. The government changed the existing law so it would have a legal ground to imprison the Japanese. Another example was the suspension of *habeas corpus* by President Abraham Lincoln during the Civil War.

16. Answers will vary.

17. In a household ruled by Roman Law your reason will fail. The parents would not care if the rules are changed without warning, and they do not care what consequences the changes may have on you. They are only concerned about how the plan benefits them. If you suffer negative consequences, it's your problem.

    In a household subject to common law, your parents would negotiate with you to select a mutually satisfactory date that would end the current allowance arrangement, at which time you would be expected to get a job outside the home. They might also caution you about making commitments which cost money, based on future earnings. The prudent action would be to first earn the money, have it in hand, then make the commitment.

18. Answers will vary.

19. The argument fails with the premise. One must agree that the emperor is given divine right to make law by the Creator. If one believes this, everything else follows naturally. Always be on guard to question the basic premise in any discussion. The logic following from the premise might be flawless, but the premise itself can be totally without evidence.

20. Answers will vary.

21. Answers will vary.

Chapter 4: Hitler and Mussolini

Define

1. Dark Ages: A period of war, economic chaos, persecution, death, destruction, ignorance, and terrible poverty. 500 A.D. to 1000 A.D.

2. Socialism: An economic and political system under which virtually everything and everyone is owned and controlled by government agencies.

Short Answer/Fill-in/True or False

3. The three stages of Roman civilization and their dates are:
   a. Roman Monarchy: 750 B.C. to 500 B.C.
   b. Roman Republic: 500 B.C. to 0
   c. Roman Empire: 0 to 500 A.D.

4. The distinguishing characteristics of each of these stages are:
   a. Roman Monarchy: statism was the system; inauguration was invented.
   b. Roman Republic: era of abundance and expansion under an early form of common law, which partly replaced statism.
   c. Roman Empire: statism returned with a vengeance; era of rampant lawmaking, welfare state, crushing taxes, runaway inflation, and war.

5. The Pax Romana began in 31 B.C., at the end of the Roman Republic, and lasted until about 170 A.D., the beginning of the Roman Empire.

6. The Pax Romana is significant because it is the period of greatest extent of the Roman Empire.

7. The Dark Ages began about 500 A.D. It marks the time when Roman civilization in Europe died. It was so horrible that scholars mourned its loss and wanted a return to Empire, to what they believed to be the source of prosperity; they did not understand it was the reason for the Dark Ages.

8. Mussolini took over Italy in three years.

9. Both Mussolini and Hitler rose to power on the promise to revive economies and make their nations great again.

10. Under fascism right and wrong are matters of opinion; rulers should do whatever appears necessary. Common law demonstrates clearly that right and wrong are not matters of opinion, and rulers must rule under the common law — not outside its bounds.

11. The two laws that are basic to all major religions of the world are: 1) do all you have agreed to do, and 2) do not encroach on other persons or their property.

12. According to Uncle Eric, the thirteen most important words you will ever read are: There is no longer any coherent system of law that is widely known.

Discussion/Essay/Assignment

13. Answers will vary.

Chapter 5: The Roman Lust for Blood

Short Answer/Fill-in/True or False

1. Uncle Eric fears the former USSR will go the way of Rome and decline into a fascist system because without the knowledge of common law, and its connection to economics, the former Soviet Empire will slide into war and a dark age because it knows of no other way to go.

2. Answers will vary.

For Further Reading

3. Suggested reading: WHATEVER HAPPENED TO JUSTICE? by Richard J. Maybury

4. Answers will vary.

Chapter 6: Logic vs. Interests

Short Answer/Fill-in/True or False

1. Governments might dislike the idea of Higher Law because it limits their power.

2. "Interests" can mean anything; it is not defined. "Interests" means carte blanche to do anything to anyone.

3. Gratian wrote DECRETUM, which restored some logic to European law and sparked the climb upward to the American Revolution, liberty, and free markets.

4. Great Depression lawmakers in most nations finally succeeded in removing the last vestiges of logic, which resurrected the Roman model (now called fascism).

Discussion/Essay/Assignment

5. Answers will vary.
6. Answers will vary.
7. Answers will vary.

Chapter 7: Listen to the Music

Short Answer/Fill-in/True or False

1. Chaostan means the land of chaos.

2. Chaostan comprises a third of all the land on earth.

3. Chaostan is inhabited by hundreds of clans, nationalities, and ethnic groups who have fought each other for hundreds of years. These people have little or no heritage of the principles of common law.

4. The country in Europe that is named after Rome is Romania.

5. For a civilization with no common law, the alternative is tyranny or chaos.

Discussion/Essay/Assignment

6. Research exercise. If desired, the student can list or identify those countries that comprise the geographical area that Uncle Eric calls Chaostan.

7. If you study, travel, or work abroad, the U.S. Government is not required to risk the lives of U.S. troops to rescue you if you get into trouble in a foreign country. Also, the rights protected by the U.S. Government for those within the U.S. borders are not extended to anyone outside the U.S. borders, which means the U.S. Government is not restrained by the safeguards of the Bill of Rights. The danger in this is that the U.S. Government can, by its treatment of foreigners on foreign soil, make many new enemies who choose to retaliate for any mistreatment they feel they may have received at the hands of the U.S. Government.

Chapter 8: The Return of Feudalism

Define

1. Serfdom: Economic slavery through heavy taxation.

Short Answer/Fill-in/True or False

2. Comparing the fall of the Roman Empire with the dissolution of the former Soviet Empire, neither had common law. They had only the law of Empire. Without a legal system based on common law, Ancient Rome and the former Soviet Empire were both left with anarchy that resulted in each Empire warring among themselves.

3. The significance of Caerphilly Castle in Wales is its size and strength of fortification demonstrating the fear its inhabitants had of its warring neighbors.

Discussion/Essay/Assignment

4. Answers will vary based on the current status of the Iraqi government at the time the student answers this question. The exercise is designed for the student to apply research skills, collect the necessary data to answer the question, and draw conclusions based on the research data. A sample answer follows, based on information about Iraq, at the time I address this question today: As I write this today, the effort in Iraq is towards democracy. Given the diverse ethnic groups that inhabit the country, democracy will result in majority rule at the expense of the minority. Political law, which does not have the safeguards and constraints of common law, will rest with the majority. The majority will vote for laws and policies that will serve their best interests at the expense of the minority which will probably result in continued ethnic dissidence.

5. Answers will vary.

Chapter 9: Straight Lines

Short Answer/Fill-in/True or False

1. Straight-line borders cut across native borders to create new borders, paying no attention to the tribal allegiances that might be split by the creation of these new borders. Borders are drawn in ways convenient to the conquerors.

2. Following the Roman model, the former Soviet Empire conquered native peoples and sent in Russians to colonize these people. With the dissolution of the former Soviet Empire, these conquered peoples declared independence. But unable to agree about the borders, wars resulted.

Discussion/Essay/Assignment

3. When the U.S. formed its states' boundaries, Native American boundaries were changed. U.S. states' borders are mostly long straight lines. Prior to European impact Native American nations did not generally have formal borders. Native American nations were generally separated by natural borders, for example, rivers, lakes, or mountains.

Chapter 10: The Byzantine Empire

Short Answer/Fill-in/True or False

1. The Roman Empire in Europe collapsed in 500 A.D., however the eastern portion, centered in what is today Turkey, continued for another thousand years and was called the Byzantine Empire.

2. Justinian tried to simplify Roman law by condensing it into 4,652 laws. These became the foundation of the Byzantine government and eventually of law across most of Europe.

3. England and Ireland were exceptions because the ocean protected them geographically, so they were more free to develop their own common law systems.

4. In Chaostan, the reason everyone is fighting for control of the government is because without control, and without common law to protect individual rights, those in power can do whatever appears necessary to promote their interests. To not be in control is to be powerless.

5. Constantinople was the capital of the Byzantine Empire. It survived because of its economic strength; it was the chokepoint for trade between Europe and the Orient. Revenues garnered from Constantinople kept the Byzantine Empire alive.

6. Christianity was the official religion of the Byzantine Empire prior to 1054 A.D.

7. In 1054 A.D. church officials in Constantinople and Rome quarreled and excommunicated each other; this split Christianity, giving us the Roman Catholic Church in the West and the Eastern Orthodox Church in the East.

8. The weakened civilization was overrun and conquered by the Ottoman Turks who were Muslim.

9. The people were told that if they became Muslims their heavy tax burdens would be cut.

10. The most disputed territories were those around the Black Sea, including Crimea and the Balkans. The Muslims had colonized these areas, and the Russians and Serbs wanted to push the Muslims out. Russia wanted free access to the Black Sea, Mediterranean, and Atlantic, but the Turks had Istanbul.

11. The lead troops of the Russians were the Cossacks who were Christian.

12. The mortal enemy of the Cossacks have been the Muslims.

13. At the beginning of the 21st century, the enemies in Bosnia, Tajikistan, the Caucasus mountains, and Georgia were:

    Bosnia: Serbs vs. Muslims
    Tajikistan: Russians vs. Muslims
    Caucasus mountains: Cossacks vs. Muslims
    Georgia: Georgians vs. Muslims

14. The significance of the groups in the preceding question is that they make up the same feud, Christians vs. Muslims, left over from the Byzantine Empire.

15. At the beginning of the 21st century, the territories that comprised the Balkans included: Slovenia, Serbia, Bosnia, Macedonia, Albania, Greece, Kosovo, Montenegro, Bulgaria, Romania, and the European part of Turkey. Second half of this question may vary, depending on current events. The point of the exercise is for the student to research to determine if there have been changes, and if so, discuss why they might have come about.

16. The two-headed eagle was the sign of the Byzantine Empire. Looking both east and west, it symbolized control of the Bosporus. Russian nationalists are reviving this symbol.

Discussion/Essay/Assignment

17. Answers will vary, but look for reasons to support the student's position, not just opinion.

18. Answers will vary, but look for reasons to support the student's position, not just opinion.

For Further Reading

19. In GEORGE WASHINGTON'S FAREWELL ADDRESS, Washington warned Americans to stay out of the political affairs of Europe because Europe is a nation of eternal wars. He supported visiting Europe and trading with Europe but cautioned Americans to avoid political connections and war with Europe. The U.S. has not heeded his warning.

Chapter 11: Summary

Short Answer/Fill-in/True or False

1. True. History can seem like a meaningless collection of facts if you do not have a model of how the world works to help you understand history and learns its lessons.

2. True. Many people mistakenly believe the Pax Romana was the good old days and try to recreate it.

3. False, the corrected statement is: The Roman model is fascism. Its only principle is that powerholders should do whatever appears necessary to achieve their goals, no exceptions and no limits.

4. Ancient Rome flourished under an early form of common law during the Roman Republic.

5. **Political** law was the root cause of the fall of Ancient Rome and the subsequent Dark Ages.

6. Some examples of Ancient Roman ideas/symbols that influence society today are: the incorporation of the fasces in architecture and on coins; the move toward statism – the philosophy of conquest and political law; unity and one-world government.

7. **Europe** has been the source of history's worst wars.

8. The Roman model is also called the Roman **disease** because **of all the bloodshed and poverty it has caused.**

9. False. The corrected statement is: The Roman model assumes political power is a good thing.

10. Fundamental to another Golden Age is a society based on a rational legal system that embraces the two fundamental laws: 1) do all you have agreed to do, and 2) do not encroach on other persons or their property.

Final Exam Answers

1. Free market economics and Higher Law are the two models Richard Maybury thinks are most reliable and also crucially important for everyone to learn.

2. **Fascism** is the political philosophy that is no philosophy at all. It embraces the concept that those in power can do whatever appears necessary to achieve their goals.

3. Juris Naturalism is the belief in a Natural Law that is higher than any government's law.

4. Ancient Rome was founded circa 750 B.C.

5. The four distinct periods that make up the rise and fall of Rome's power are: Roman Monarchy, Roman Republic, Pax Romana, and the Roman Empire.

6. Roman power was at its peak during the Pax Romana.

7. The Roman Disease is statism, the assumption that laws can be made up by human lawmakers.

8. In Ancient Rome, fasces was a bundle of wooden rods bound together by red-colored bands, fixed to a wooden pole that was topped by an ax. The fasces symbolized the unification of the people under a single government.

9. Statism assumes political power is a good thing and everyone should have some. Under statism, government is our friend, our protector, the solution to our problems. Force is the tool for enforcement. There is no law higher than the government's law. Statism is the opposite of the original American philosophy.

10. Investment values are mostly determined by trends in the economy; trends in the economy are mostly determined by politics.

11. Common law is the system for discovering and applying the Natural Laws that determine the results of human behavior. Common law is the system for discovering and applying the Natural Laws that govern the human ecology. The body of definitions and precedents growing from the two fundamental laws that make civilization possible are: (1) do all you have agreed to do, and (2) do not encroach on other persons or their property.

12. There are no restraints on a government that practices Roman law. If government can make up law, it can pass whatever laws it wants to justify whatever actions it wants to take.

13. The distinguishing characteristics of each of these stages are:
    a. Roman Monarchy: statism was the system; inauguration was invented.
    b. Roman Republic: era of abundance and expansion under an early form of common law, which partly replaced statism.
    c. Roman Empire: statism returned with a vengeance; era of rampant lawmaking, welfare state, crushing taxes, runaway inflation, and war.

14. The Dark Ages began about 500 A.D. It marks the time when Roman civilization in Europe died. It was so horrible that scholars mourned its loss and wanted a return to Empire, to what they believed to be the source of prosperity; they did not understand this Empire was the reason for the Dark Ages.

15. "Interests" can mean anything; it is not defined. "Interests" means carte blanche to do anything to anyone.

16. Great Depression lawmakers in most nations finally succeeded in removing the last vestiges of logic, which resurrected the Roman model, which is now called fascism.

17. Chaostan means the land of chaos.

18. Chaostan is inhabited by hundreds of clans, nationalities, and ethnic groups who have fought each other for hundreds of years. These people have little or no heritage of the principles of common law.

19. For a civilization with no common law, the alternative is tyranny or chaos.

20. Serfdom: Economic slavery through heavy taxation.

21. Straight-line borders cut across native borders to create new borders, paying no attention to the tribal allegiances that might be split by the creation of these new borders. Borders are drawn in ways convenient to the conquerors.

22. The Roman Empire in Europe collapsed in 500 A.D., however the eastern portion, centered in what is today Turkey, continued for another thousand years and was called the Byzantine Empire.

23. England and Ireland were exceptions because the ocean protected each geographically, so each was more free to develop its own common law systems.

24. Christianity was the official religion of the Byzantine Empire prior to 1054 A.D.

25. The weakened Byzantine civilization was overrun and conquered by the Ottoman Turks, who were Muslim.

Answers

26. At the beginning of the 21st century, the enemies in Bosnia, Tajikistan, the Caucasus mountains, and Georgia were:

    Bosnia: Serbs vs. Muslims
    Tajikistan: Russians vs. Muslims
    Caucasus mountains: Cossacks vs. Muslims
    Georgia: Georgians vs. Muslims

27. False. The corrected statement is: The Roman model is fascism. Its only principle is that powerholders should do whatever appears necessary to achieve their goals, no exceptions and no limits.

28. Fundamental to another Golden Age is a society based on a rational legal system that embraces the two fundamental laws: 1) do all you have agreed to do, and 2) do not encroach on other persons or their property.

29. False. The corrected statement is: Scientific law is based on fact, logic, and the two fundamental laws: 1) do all you have agreed to do, and 2) do not encroach on other persons or their property.

30. False. The corrected statement is: Scientific law is cautious and hesitant in the use of force.

31. True. Scientific law is predictable and knowable.

32. True. Political law is made up by politicians.

33. **Scientific** law tends to neutralize political power. **Political** law gives powerseekers more power.

34. **Political** law uses force to redistribute wealth and destroys incentive to produce wealth.

35. False. The corrected statement is: Scientific law makes effective economic calculations.

36. Essays will vary.

Published by Bluestocking Press

Uncle Eric Books by Richard J. Maybury

- UNCLE ERIC TALKS ABOUT PERSONAL, CAREER, AND FINANCIAL SECURITY
- WHATEVER HAPPENED TO PENNY CANDY?
- WHATEVER HAPPENED TO JUSTICE?
- ARE YOU LIBERAL? CONSERVATIVE? OR CONFUSED?
- ANCIENT ROME: HOW IT AFFECTS YOU TODAY
- EVALUATING BOOKS: WHAT WOULD THOMAS JEFFERSON THINK ABOUT THIS?
- THE MONEY MYSTERY
- THE CLIPPER SHIP STRATEGY
- THE THOUSAND YEAR WAR IN THE MIDEAST
- WORLD WAR I: THE REST OF THE STORY
- WORLD WAR II: THE REST OF THE STORY

Bluestocking Guides (study guides for the Uncle Eric books)
by Jane A. Williams and/or Kathryn Daniels

- A BLUESTOCKING GUIDE: BUILDING A PERSONAL MODEL FOR SUCCESS
- A BLUESTOCKING GUIDE: ECONOMICS (based on WHATEVER HAPPENED TO PENNY CANDY?)
- A BLUESTOCKING GUIDE: JUSTICE (based on WHATEVER HAPPENED TO JUSTICE?)
- A BLUESTOCKING GUIDE: POLITICAL PHILOSOPHIES (based on ARE YOU LIBERAL? CONSERVATIVE? OR CONFUSED?)
- A BLUESTOCKING GUIDE: ANCIENT ROME
- A BLUESTOCKING GUIDE: SOLVING THE MONEY MYSTERY
- A BLUESTOCKING GUIDE: APPLYING THE CLIPPER SHIP STRATEGY [available Winter, 2004]
- A BLUESTOCKING GUIDE: THE MIDEAST WAR (based on THE THOUSAND YEAR WAR IN THE MIDEAST) [available Spring, 2005]
- A BLUESTOCKING GUIDE: WORLD WAR I: THE REST OF THE STORY [available Winter, 2004]
- A BLUESTOCKING GUIDE: WORLD WAR II: THE REST OF THE STORY [available Winter, 2004]

Each Study Guide includes some or all of the following:
1) chapter-by-chapter comprehension questions and answers
2) application questions and answers
3) research activities
4) essay assignments
5) thought questions
6) final exam

More Bluestocking Press Titles

- LAURA INGALLS WILDER AND ROSE WILDER LANE HISTORICAL TIMETABLE
- ECONOMICS: A FREE MARKET READER edited by Jane Williams & Kathryn Daniels
- CAPITALISM FOR KIDS: GROWING UP TO BE YOUR OWN BOSS by Karl Hess [available Winter, 2004]
- BUSINESS: IT'S ALL ABOUT COMMON SENSE by Kathryn Daniels and Anthony Joseph [available Spring, 2005]

The Bluestocking Press Catalog includes varied and interesting selections of history products: historical toys and crafts, historical documents, historical fiction, primary sources, and more.

Order any of the above items from Bluestocking Press by phone or online.

Bluestocking Press
Phone: 800-959-8586
email: CustomerService@BluestockingPress.com
web site: www.BluestockingPress.com